W9-BKN-010

The PROJECT LETTERING Book

Robert Ainsworth

SCHOLASTIC INC.

New York Toronto London Auckland Sydney
Mexico City New Delhi Hong Kong

Dedicated to my five children,
Nadan, Lara, Rowan, Merribeth and Bronton,
who contributed some of the ideas for this book.

No part of this publication may be reproduced in whole or in part, or stored in a
retrieval system, or transmitted in any form or by any means, electronic, mechanical,
photocopying, recording, or otherwise, without written permission of the publisher.
For information regarding permission, write to
Scholastic Australia Pty Limited ACN 000 614 577, PO Box 579, Gosford 2250.

ISBN 0-439-10844-6

Copyright © 1994 by Robert Ainsworth. All rights reserved.
Published by Scholastic Inc., 555 Broadway, New York, NY 10012, by arrangement
with Scholastic Australia Pty Limited. SCHOLASTIC and associated logos are
trademarks and/or registered trademarks of Scholastic Inc.

12 11 10 9 8 7 6 5 4 3 2   9/9 0 1 2 3 4/0

Printed in the U.S.A.   08

First Scholastic printing, October 1999

Typeset by Proset Imaging, Forresters Beach NSW.

CONTENTS

About this Book

The idea for this book was born in a classroom while I was preparing a spelling lesson for a group of Year 7 students.

I doctored-up the words a bit to make them look like what they meant.

The students were excited about what we could do with words—just by using a bit of imagination and having a sense of fun.

I'm sure you will be as excited as they were!

In this book I've given you lots of examples to help you get started.

HAVE FUN!

Robert Ainsworth

*T*hese are the twelve 'dull and boring' words which I had to teach to my Year 7 class. Here are the original ideas I used to bring the words to life, to try to make the task of remembering what they meant—and how to spell them—easier.

 **NOW...** Let's try some simple words— straight out of the Dictionary.

- BABY
- BAD
- BADGE
- BAG
- BAKE
- BALANCE
- BALD
- BALE
- BALL
- BALLOON
- BAMBOO
- BANANA
- BANG
- BANK
- BANNER

Let's see what we can do with them...

I wonder how much we can do with **ONE** word...?

We'll need to pick a word that reminds us of lots of things.

Let's see .... **BEACH!** That's a good word.

There are lots of things to see at the seaside.
We can use them to take the place of some of the letters in the word "BEACH."

Things like...

BEACH (×27, each stylized with beach-themed lettering and illustrations)

8

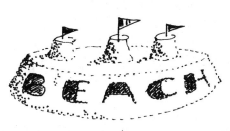

As you can see... the sky is the limit with what you can do with words!

Here are some "C"s...

- CAB
- CABBAGE
- CABIN
- CABLE
- CACTUS
- CAGE
- CAKE
- CAMP

...words galore...

STRIPES

ROSE ROSE PIN

FENCE FENCE FENCE

FACE Faces Bubble

OPEN - SHUT BRANCH

DRESS STONE ROCK

HIGH EMPTY HOLD-UP

HOSE   DiffeReNt

TRaP   CLOMP

LEAF   DISAPPEAR   ROOF

WOOL   ARTIST   Puddle

GOLF   IGNITE   STRICT

SIGN   WHEELS   BUMPED

Travel   Grab   EAGLE

Here's a **FUN** word!

Let's do some **Face** EXPRESSION words...

Happy SAD GROWL

FROWN Laugh CRY

Grump Groan Asleep

scowl Grin SHOUT

FLIRT smile BLOW

chew Bite cringe

15

How about BODY PARTS...

Head NOSE SKULL

FACE NOSE eyes

MOUTH cheeks chin

Tongue TEETH ears

Beard Neck Hair

16

More... **BODY PARTS**

LIPS Freckles HAIR

Jaw Moustache HAIR

Toe FEET Leg

TUMMY ANKLE BOTTOM

ARM Brain BONE

... FOR PROJECTS

AMERICA

Geography of Australia

MY VISIT TO PARIS

FISH OF The World

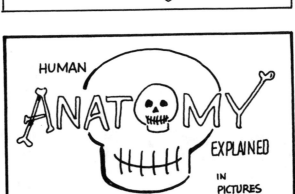

HUMAN ANATOMY EXPLAINED IN PICTURES

OUR EXCURSION TO THE BEACH

MOUNTAIN RANGES IN ASIA

SOME OF THE BIG ANIMALS OF THE WORLD

WOOL GROWING in New Zealand

A good way to come up with ideas for your project title is to think of the **OBJECTS** the title reminds you of.

 For example...

IN THIS CASE THE **OBJECT** IS THE SHEAF OF WHEAT — BUT NOTICE ALSO THE BIRDS AND CLOUDS WHICH ADD ATMOSPHERE.

You can even make the <u>whole</u> word into an object.

 For example...

AGAIN... ADD THE SUN AND BIRDS AND HORIZON. THESE HELP TO ESTABLISH A SENSE OF <u>PLACE</u>.

Another very good way to generate ideas is to think of the **ACTION** the title reminds you of.

 For example...

HARVEST

Don't forget, you can turn the letters into **BODY PARTS**.

This can be very useful because body parts — or even whole bodies — can portray **ACTION** as well.

Examples...

RUN

COMMUNICATION

You can even use animals...

Birds

Quack

Pets

Put your ideas to good USE FOR SIGNS ...

Buy your HOT CHIPS at the ...

Canteen

Tea and Coffee

50¢ a cup

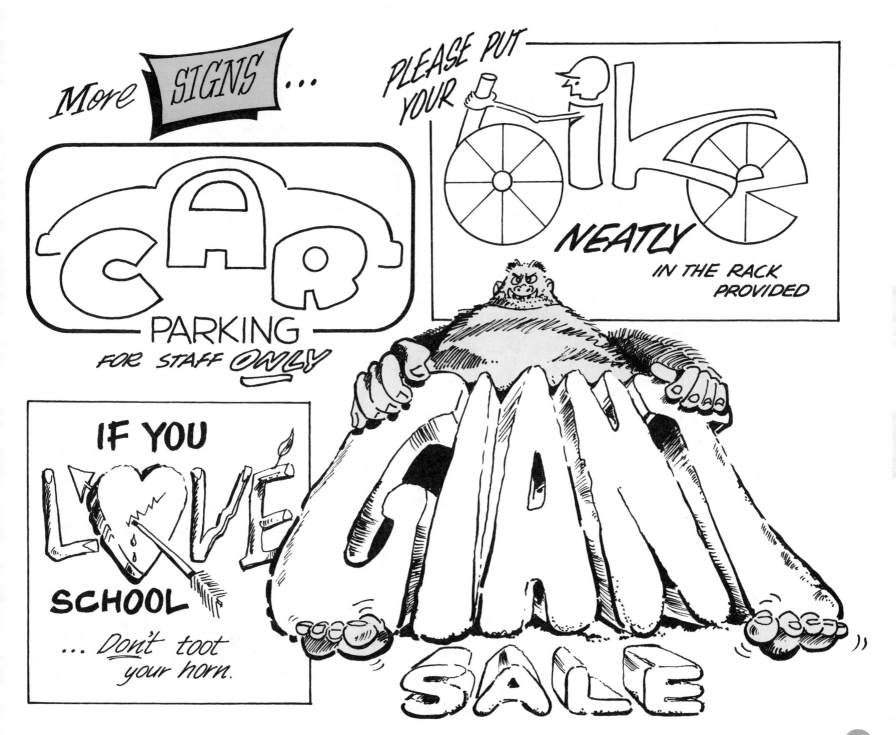

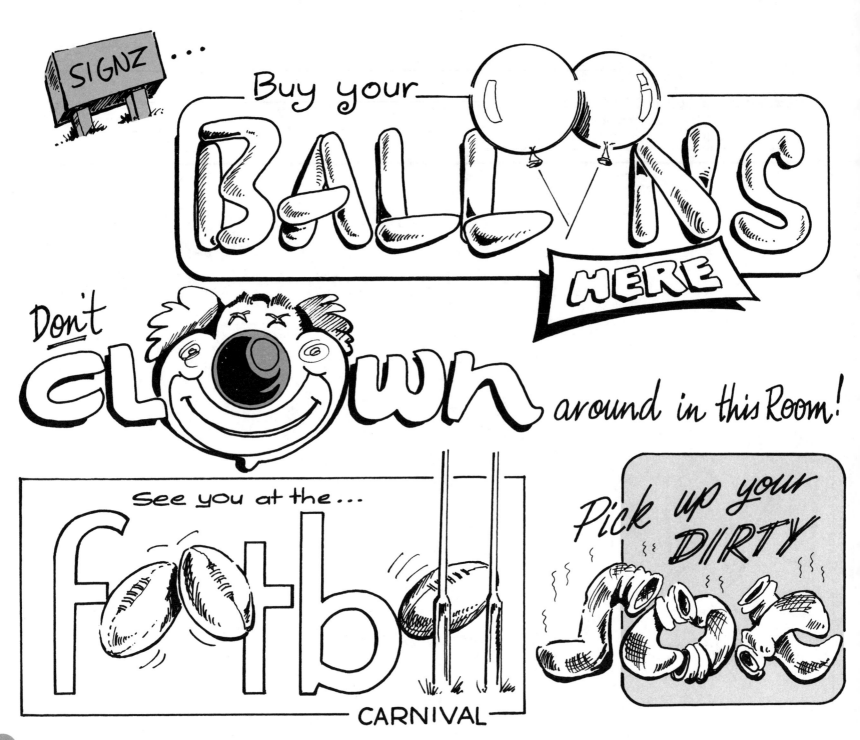

SIGNZ ...

Buy your BALLOONS HERE

Don't CLOWN around in this Room!

See you at the ... FOOTBALL CARNIVAL

Pick up your DIRTY SOX

SIGNS

Please sit on your CHAIR PROPERLY

Please REPLACE THE LID ON THE Toothpaste

PLEASE SHUT the DOOR
THANK YOU

Lemonade FOR SALE HERE

MIND THE STEPS

SIGNS

Ribbon

BRIDAL WEAR

Summer fashions

AUTUMN SHADES

SPRING FEVER

WINTER SALE

Try some....

GEOMETRY Terms

ROUND SQUARE OBLONG

OVAL TRIANGLE DOT

PYRAMID Hexagon

BLOCK Parallelogram

CONE DIAMOND RHOMBUS

TRAPESIUM PENTAGON

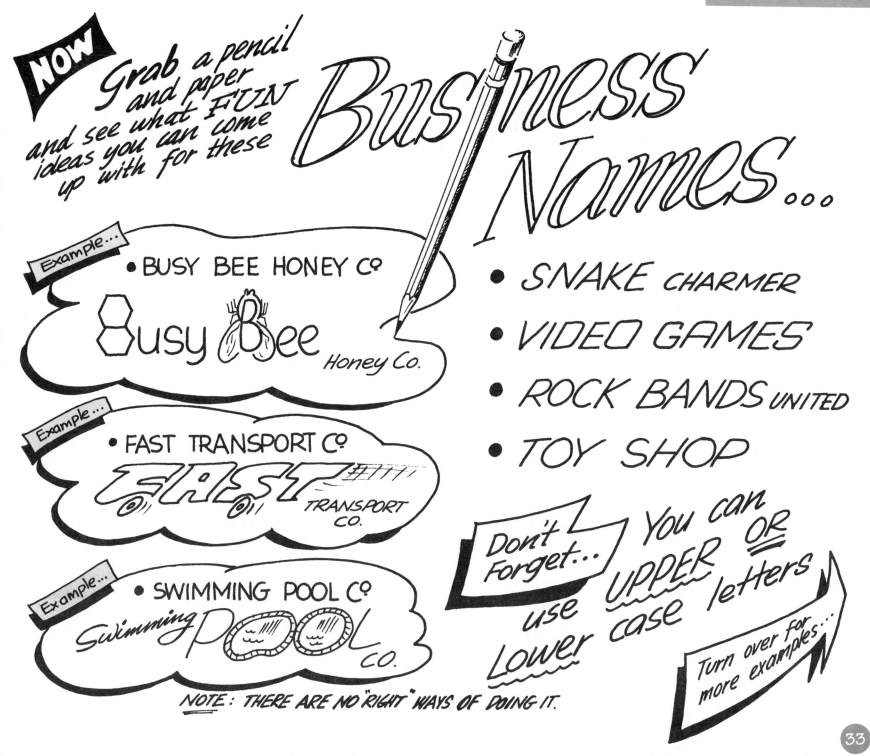

Use these to trigger your imagination...

HORSe GROOMERS LTD.

U.R. SICK BANDAGE CO. LTD.

BIG OVERLAND TOURS INC.

BOAT SKI CLUB SUPPLIES

LOG TIMBER YARD

Proprietor: HOLLY WOOD

RICH & SON PTY. LTD. BANKERS

Digger BONE & Co.
ARCHAEOLOGISTS

Toothpick EMPORIUM
Proprietor: CHEW CELERY & Co.

Al Lee Cat & Co.
PET SHOP

TAP DANGER FOR HIRE

X.S. Smoke & Co.
MANUFACTURERS

AIRPORT JOY-RIDE Co.

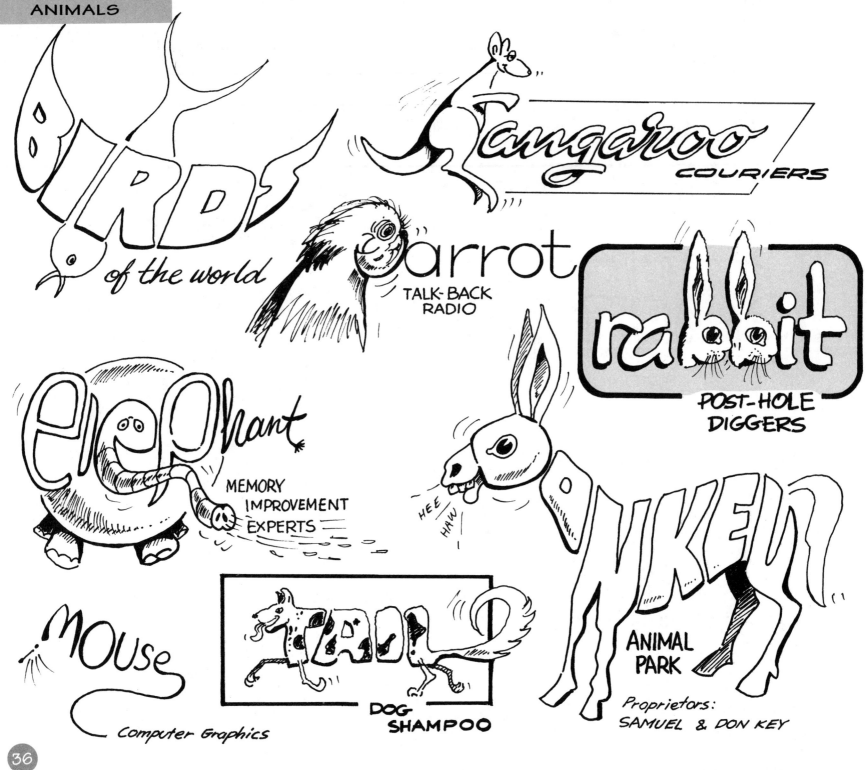

BIRDS
of the world

arrot
TALK-BACK
RADIO

Kangaroo
COURIERS

rabbit
POST-HOLE
DIGGERS

eLePhant
MEMORY
IMPROVEMENT
EXPERTS

HEE
HAW

DONKEY
ANIMAL
PARK

Proprietors:
SAMUEL & DON KEY

MOUSe
Computer Graphics

POODLE
DOG
SHAMPOO

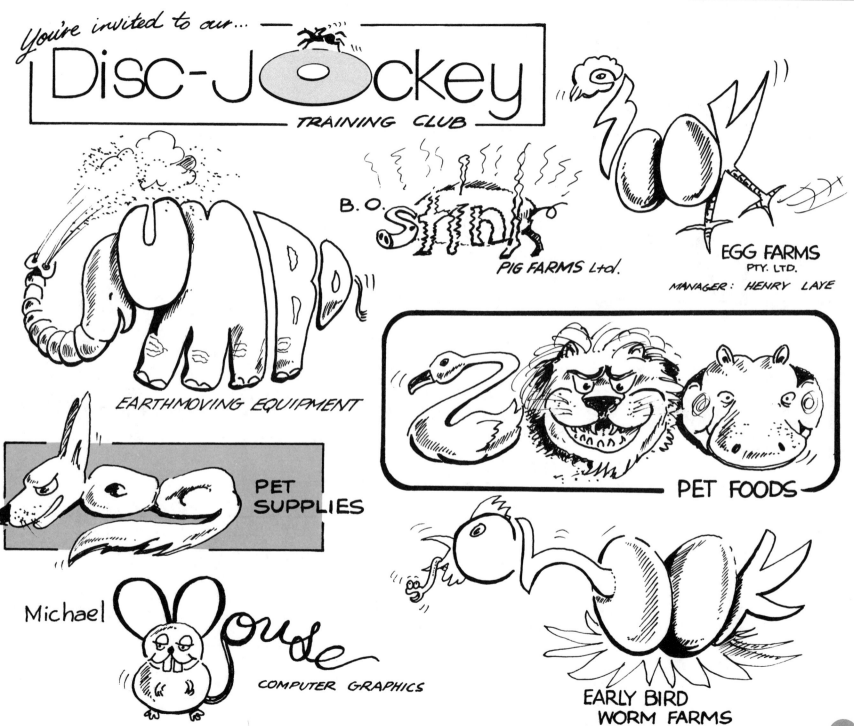

You're invited to our...

Disc-Jockey
TRAINING CLUB

EARTHMOVING EQUIPMENT

B.O. Stink
PIG FARMS Ltd.

EGG FARMS
PTY. LTD.
MANAGER: HENRY LAYE

PET
SUPPLIES

PET FOODS

Michael Mouse
COMPUTER GRAPHICS

EARLY BIRD
WORM FARMS

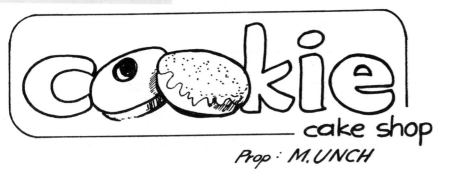

cake shop

Prop: M.UNCH

Vineyard

WINE - TASTING

Take-away
FOOD

Proprietor: M.T. TUMM

FUNNY "HA-HA

Cafe

PROP: PHYLLIS UPP

LEAVE YOUR

FAST FOOD

Prop.: Harry Upp.

ICECREAM C°

PROPRIETORS:
PHILIP & ANITA.

TOFFEE

LOLLIE SHOP

Lunch BAR

Prop: Sam Vich.

COOK up a Feast with...

BANANA

MONKEY BUSINESS FOODS

See you at the... **SALT** & **pepp** ACHOO!

Restaurant

FOR HOME-STYLE COOKING

D. LISIOUS
Fruit & Vegies CO. LTD.

E. CLAIR — baker PASTRYCOOK

coffee shop
Prop: Mr Bean

Dinah's CUTLERY Carvery

Caf LUNCH BAR

E.T. Lollies! TOOTHBRUSH CO.

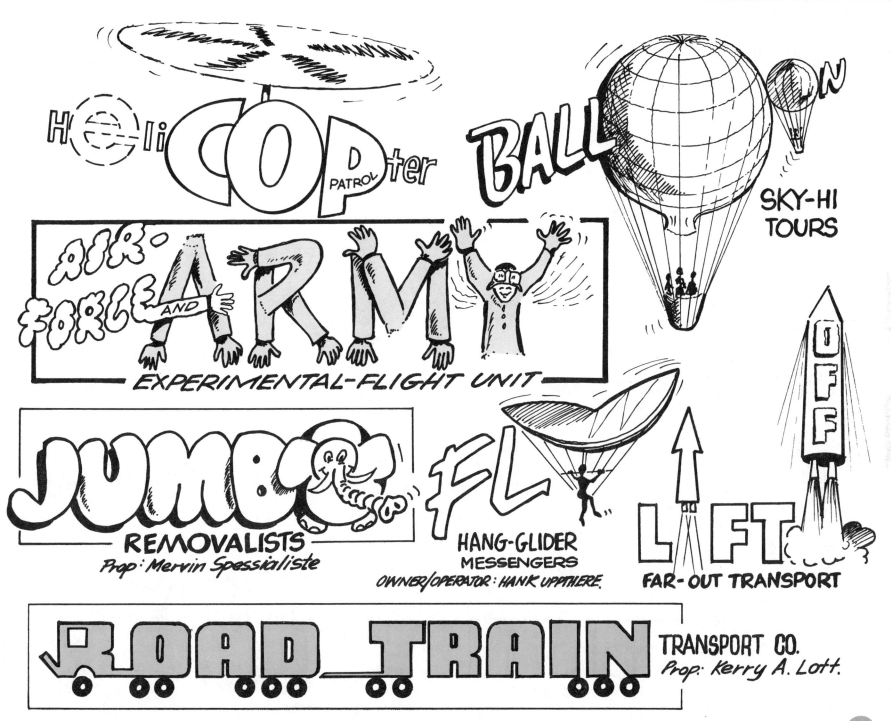

HeliCOPter PATROL

BALLOON
SKY-HI TOURS

AIR-FORCE and ARMY
EXPERIMENTAL-FLIGHT UNIT

JUMBO REMOVALISTS
Prop: Mervin Spessialiste

FLY
HANG-GLIDER MESSENGERS
OWNER/OPERATOR: HANK UPPTHERE.

LIFT OFF
FAR-OUT TRANSPORT

ROAD TRAIN TRANSPORT CO.
Prop: Kerry A. Lott.

41

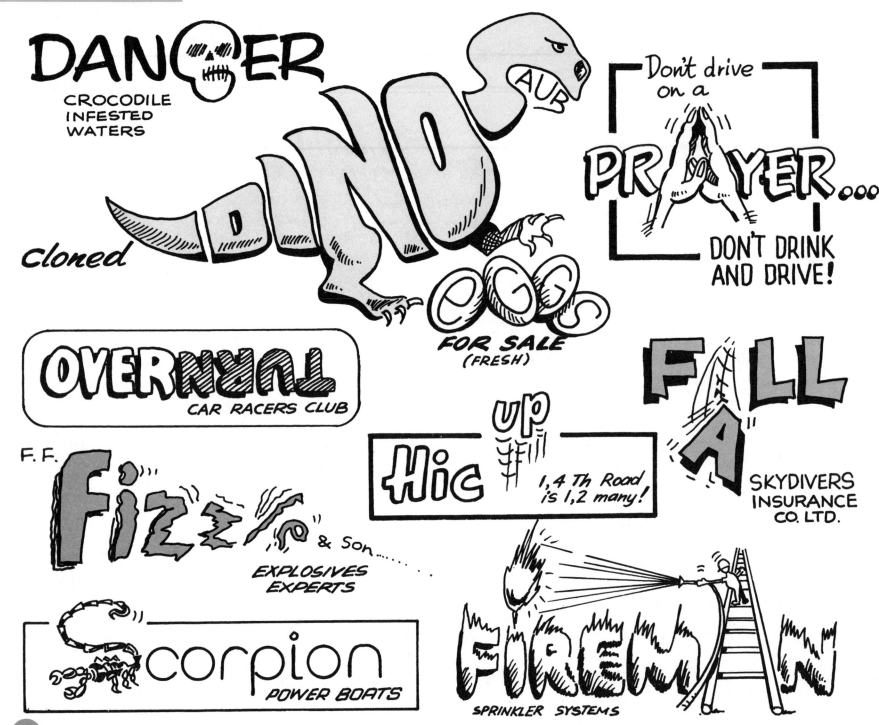

DANGER
CROCODILE
INFESTED
WATERS

Cloned DINOSAUR

EGGS
FOR SALE
(FRESH)

Don't drive
on a
PRAYER...
DON'T DRINK
AND DRIVE!

OVERTURN
CAR RACERS CLUB

FALL
SKYDIVERS
INSURANCE
CO. LTD.

F.F. Fizzr & Son........
EXPLOSIVES
EXPERTS

HiC up
1,4 Th Road
is 1,2 many!

Scorpion
POWER BOATS

FIREMAN
SPRINKLER SYSTEMS

BUTCHER
PRICE CUTTERS*
* WE'LL MEAT YOU HALF WAY.

BELL
CAR THIEF
ALARMS

W. TWIN
& PARTNER
Double Agents

FRIDGE
PEACE
WAR NEGOTIATORS

ARROW
ARCHERY CLUB

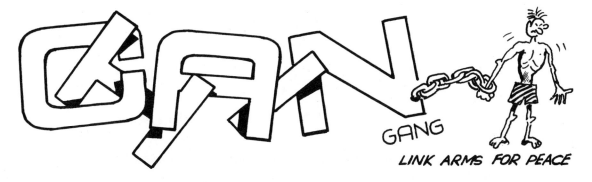

CHAIN
GANG
LINK ARMS FOR PEACE

CROSS
WORD
PUZZLES
INC.

FEAR

PHOBIA ASSOCIATION INC.

PRESIDENT: A. FRED OVEVRITHING.

DENTIST VISIT

O. PENN-WYDE M.D.
IN ASSOCIATION WITH
I. HERCHEW T.E.Th.

YELL

COMMUNICATION SYSTEMS

COMICAL NOVELTY CO.

Manager: JOE KERR

POKE

STIRRERS INTERNATIONAL Inc.

bright

OPTIMISTS CLUB!

PRESIDENT: GINGER (BLUE) SKYES.

GR**O**WL
COMPLAINTS
DEPARTMENT
Manager : LIONEL PHYTBACH

Grin
PHOTOGRAPHERS
CLUB
PRESIDENT : MONA LISA.

I.M. Grumpy & Co.
INSOMNIA CONSULTANTS

argue
U. & I. and Company

VOLCANO
ANGER MANAGEMENT CONSULTANTS
MANAGER : HELEN BACK

E.T. feed & ASSOC.
APPETITE RESTORERS

A. l⬤ner
BOUNDARY RIDER.

I. M.

& ASSOC.

PROTEST MARCHERS
CONGLOMERATE

SOUP CO.

PESSIMISTS
ASSOCIATION

THERAPY
GUILD

PHONE
SYSTEMS

YAK!
YAK!
YAK!

C. LEE & Co.

NOVELTIES

with Patrick Ortreat & Assoc.

M.T.

PSYCHIATRISTS

MANAGER: LOLA BOUTE

I.

& CO.

CHILD PSYCHOLOGISTS

GLASS & CO.

SMASH &
GRAB
SPECIALISTS

NICK YORWALLET

"Fingers" & ACCOMPLICE

PICKPOCKETS

PRISONER

Penfriends Inc.

SHERLOCK

MAGNIFY & PARTNER

PRIVATE DETECTIVES

X.X.

robber & Partners

ANTIQUE
COLLECTORS
&
JEWELLERS

POLICE

'ere specialists

SHADOW

DETECTIVES & NIGHTWATCHMENS
CLUB

SECURITY

UNDER-ARM DEODORANT

SECURITY GUARDS

LIARS CLUB Inc.

SECRETARY : IDA DOWNE

SCANDAL INVESTIGATORS GUILD

FRED *Thread* & Assoc.

PRIVATE DETECTIVES

IN ASSOCIATION WITH ESAU U. DOIT & CO.

BURGLAR ALARMS

SECURITY ALARMS

PRISONER REHABILITATION SERVICES

Sea Gull
HANG-GLIDER CLUB

FLOAT
BANKERS

U. Can
Swim & Co.
SWIMMING CLASSES

SAVE the WHALES
EAT YOUR VEGIES!

JAWS
DIVING EQUIPMENT

LIGHTHOUSE MARINE
SAFETY PRODUCTS

diver
STOCK MARKET PREDICTORS
Manager: Mark Ed. Krash.

Kissors *Hairdressers*

Hammer CARPENTERS

E.Z.

Curl

HAIRDRESSERS
Manager: CARL E. LOCKE

Electricity Suppliers & Installers

Manager: S. PARK.

Will

Saw & Son CARPENTERS

Spot on - Spot off

WINDOW CLEANERS

Snowman AIR-CONDITIONING EXPERTS

Harry

Beard BARBER

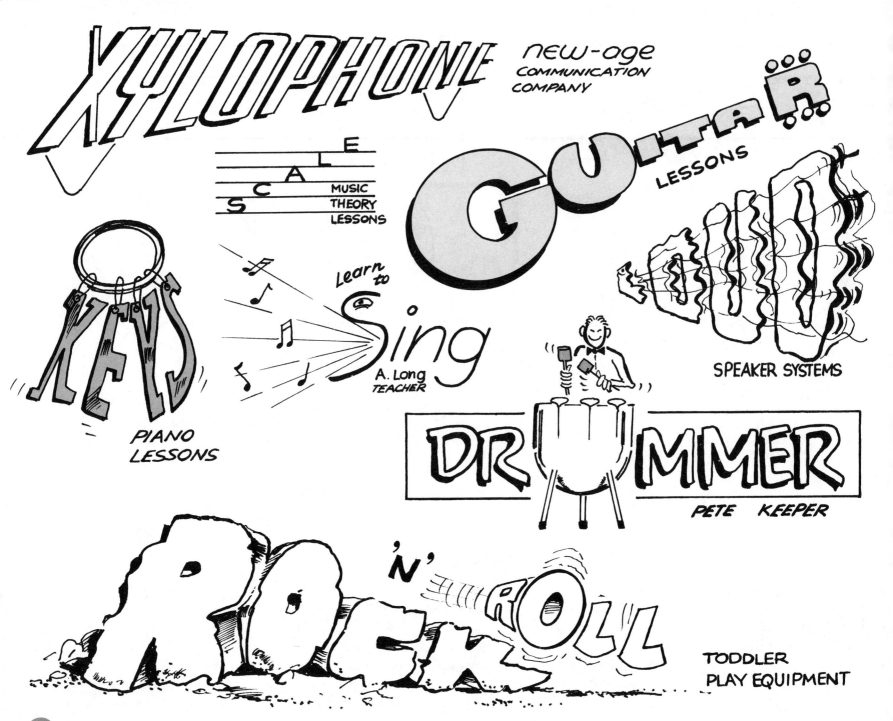

XYLOPHONE

new-age
communication
company

GUITAR

LESSONS

SCALE

MUSIC
THEORY
LESSONS

SPEAKER SYSTEMS

KEYS

Learn to Sing

A. Long
TEACHER

PIANO
LESSONS

DRUMMER

PETE KEEPER

ROCK 'N' ROLL

TODDLER
PLAY EQUIPMENT

BRUSH *Painters*
THEATRE BACKDROPS A SPECIALTY

ART Supplies

Hello **STATU?**

Q.T. **LIP STICK**
COSMETIC MAKE-UP SERVICES

Tracy **COMPASS**
DRAFTSPERSON

U. KEN **DRAW** &Co.
ART SUPPLIES

PAINTER
& DECORATOR

T shirt
ADVERTISING AGENTS

53

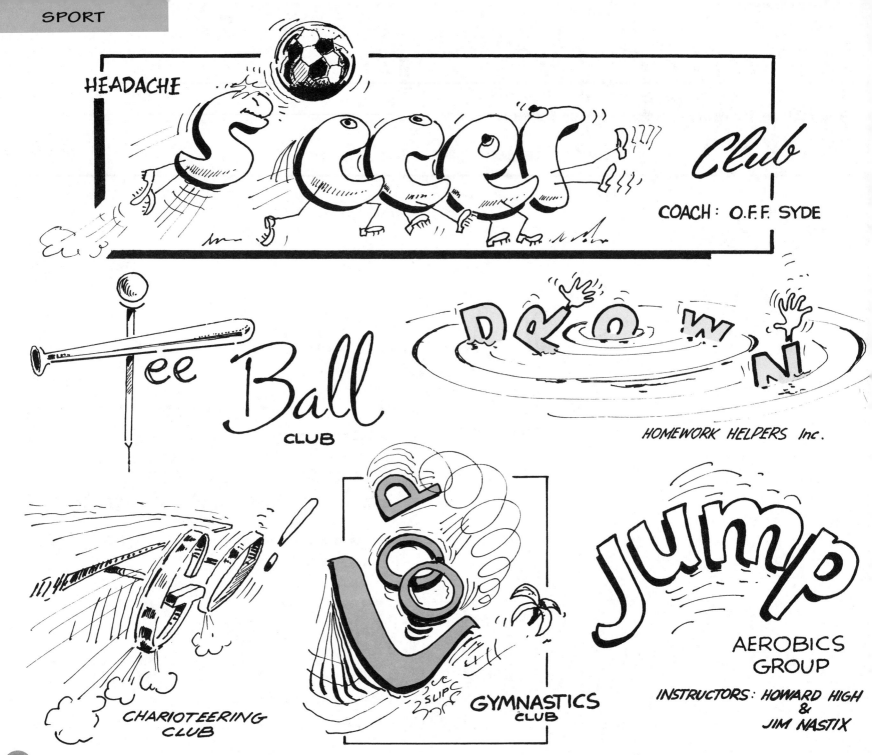

HEADACHE

SOCCER Club

COACH: O.F.F. SYDE

Tee Ball CLUB

DROWN

HOMEWORK HELPERS Inc.

CHARIOTEERING CLUB

LOOP
SLIP
GYMNASTICS CLUB

JUMP
AEROBICS GROUP

INSTRUCTORS: HOWARD HIGH & JIM NASTIX

eerball CLUB
COACH: CHUCK INN

HOOP
EXAM & TEST COACHERS
HEAD TEACHER: MARK HARD.

hop-in Deli
Prop: Carmen U.R. Velcum

jaw
BOXING GLOVE SUPPLIES

U.L. stip & Co.Ltd.
FLOOR POLISHERS

ouch COURIERS

Hb
SPORTS EQUIPMENT

TIRED
FITNESS CLUB

55

End the **TORTURE** at the Gym.

... PLAY LAWN BOWLS instead!

Avoid **INJURY** ... PLAY CHESS instead!

DANCER SPECIALIST SHOES

SLIDE WORLD ECONOMIC SUMMIT

HOWZAT **CRICKET** CLUB

FEED ME!

SURF BOARDS

WALK

HIKING EQUIPMENT

Tiptoe

& ASSOC.

MOTIVATION
EXPERTS

GONE & Co.
BACK IN 10 MINUTES

C.U....

STRIDE

HIKERS
FOOTWEAR

TRAMPOLINE

CHEQUE BOUNCERS
CO-OPERATIVE

Pan

CAMPING
SUPPLIES

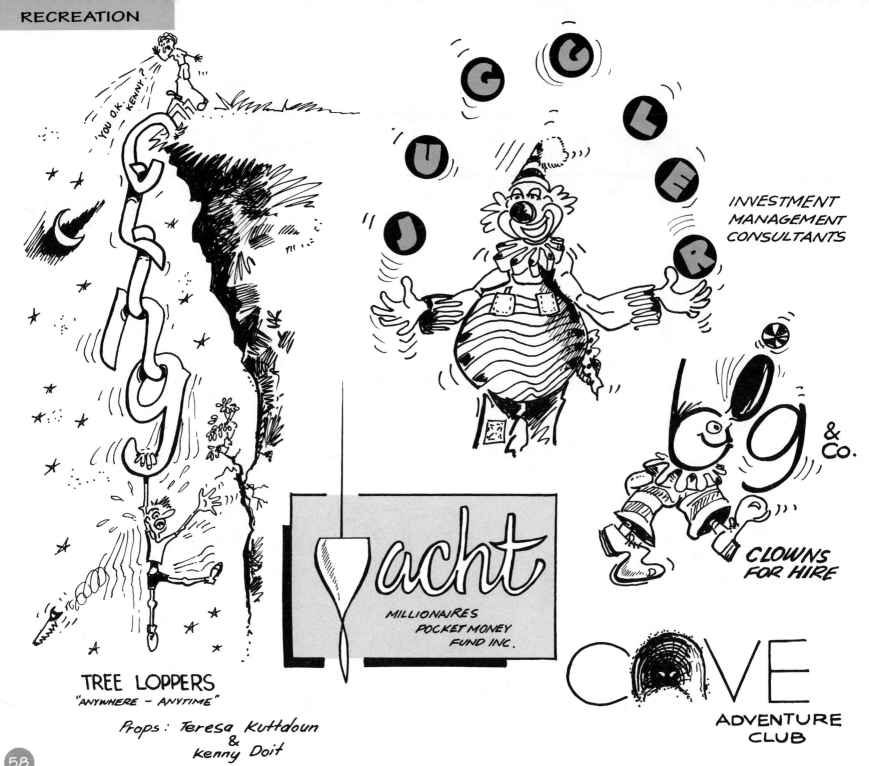

YOU O.K. KENNY?

JUGGLER

INVESTMENT MANAGEMENT CONSULTANTS

bg & Co.

CLOWNS FOR HIRE

Yacht

MILLIONAIRES POCKET MONEY FUND INC.

TREE LOPPERS
"ANYWHERE – ANYTIME"

Props: Teresa Kuttdoun & Kenny Doit

COVE
ADVENTURE CLUB

58

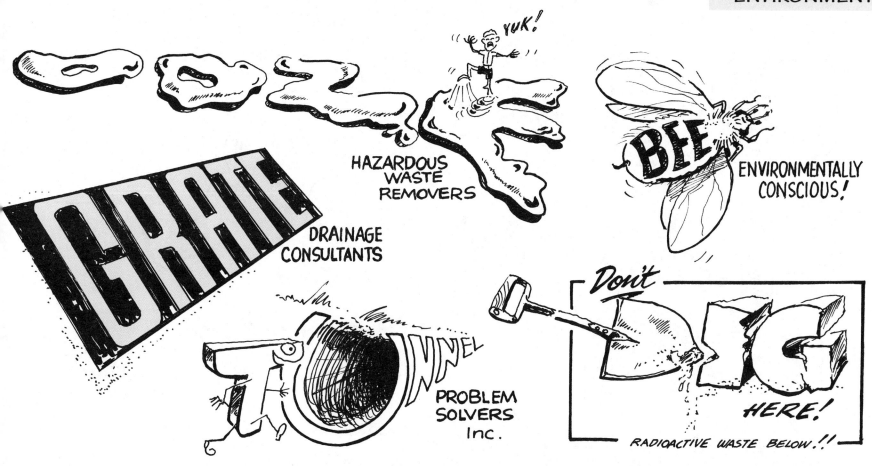

OOZE *YUK!*

HAZARDOUS
WASTE
REMOVERS

BEE
ENVIRONMENTALLY
CONSCIOUS!

GRATE
DRAINAGE
CONSULTANTS

TUNNEL
PROBLEM
SOLVERS
Inc.

Don't DIG HERE!
RADIOACTIVE WASTE BELOW.!!

CRAWL & Sons
SEWER-PIPE CLEANERS

population
CENSUS COLLECTORS
CONSORTIUM
Ltd.

spit
RETICULATION
INSTALLERS

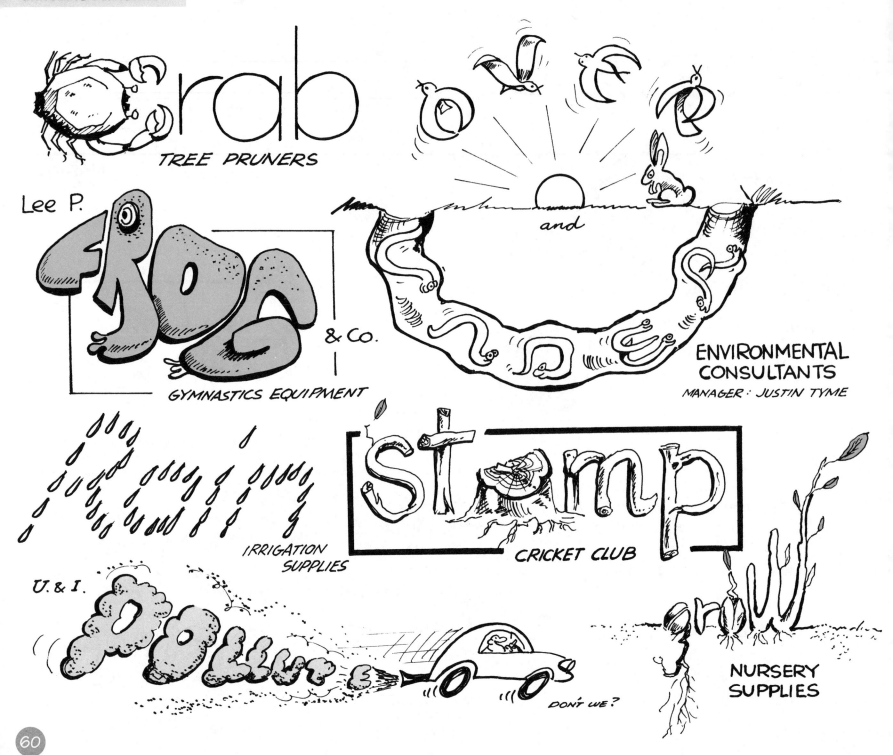

Crab
TREE PRUNERS

Lee P.
FROG & Co.
GYMNASTICS EQUIPMENT

and

ENVIRONMENTAL CONSULTANTS
MANAGER : JUSTIN TYME

IRRIGATION SUPPLIES

Stomp
CRICKET CLUB

U. & I. Pollute
DON'T WE?

grow
NURSERY SUPPLIES

Orchard
Prop: Cherry Ripe

AXE
BUDGET PLANNERS COMMITTEE

Umbrella & SON
WEATHER FORECASTERS

Vent
FRESH AIR CONTROL SYSTEMS LTD.

Teresa Downe & Co.
PAPER
MERCHANT

junk yard
Manager: CHUCK OUTTE

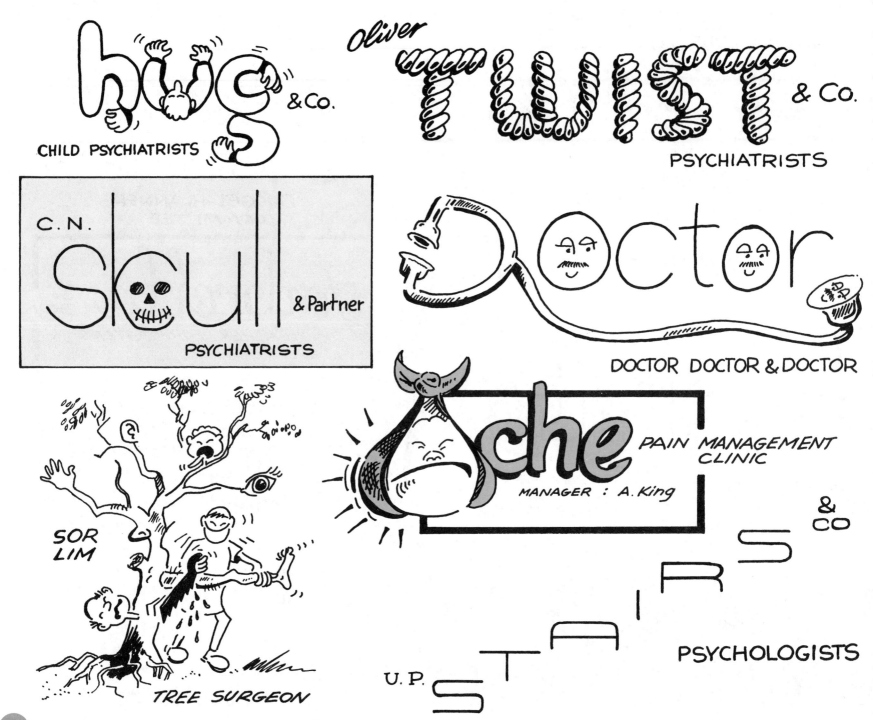

hug & Co.
CHILD PSYCHIATRISTS

Oliver TWIST & Co.
PSYCHIATRISTS

C.N. Skull & Partner
PSYCHIATRISTS

Doctor
DOCTOR DOCTOR & DOCTOR

Ache PAIN MANAGEMENT CLINIC
MANAGER : A. King

SOR LIM
TREE SURGEON

U.P. STAIRS & CO
PSYCHOLOGISTS

To trigger your ideas, just think of

OBJECTS

and ACTION

This will help you bring your projects to life